*"Hi," cooed the peace dove,*
*through the windows of the cage,*
*"from nature with love."*

# VIRAL ODES

# Viral Odes

*Pandemic Poems — a souvenir of a unique year*

## Sharron Green

An Ink Gladiators Press® Publication

## Ink Gladiators Press®
*Publishing and promoting warriors on life's battlefield*

Ink Gladiators Press is an ePublishing company whose mission is to publish and promote writers, poets, lyricists, artists and photographers through our current worldwide market distribution of over 3 billion readership. It is not affiliated with any other organization and is an independent ePublishing house. For Earthians who want to publish with us, check out our ongoing publishing opportunities at Our Earthians Community Group and Translations Of Hope, or write to us to learn more about our high-end professional Celestial Sky Services at our email address: contact@inkgladiatorspress.com.
Bangalore 560077, India
www.inkgladiatorspress.com

First Edition
Copyright © Sharron Green 2020

## Viral Odes

ISBN: 978-1-7396617-0-0

Credits:
Photography: Sharron Green
Designer - Leonie Belle Hawk
Editor - Reena Doss

All rights reserved. This edition can only be distributed by the publisher and author. This book is the work of the author's perceptions, observations and insights and are based on her individual experiences. No reference to any real person is intended or should be inferred. The moral rights of the author and publisher have been asserted. No part of this book may be reproduced in any form, on or by electronic or mechanical means, including information storage and retrieval systems, without permission in writing from the publisher and author, with the only exception being made for a reviewer who may quote brief passages in a review. Disclaimer: Any views or opinions expressed by the author are personal and do not represent those of Ink Gladiators Press, any of its staff, communities or affiliates unless explicitly stated.

*Poet of a certain age,
jotting rhymes upon the page,
sharing thoughts on 2020,
a year that has challenged plenty.*

*Thanks to friends and family,
for all support given to me
through these pandemonic days
living in a lockdown haze.*

*Sharron Green © Photography*

# Author's Note

*Dear Readers,*

*As you may be aware, Britain went into lockdown on March 23rd 2020 and Viral Odes is a direct consequence of the subsequent months in isolation during this global tragedy. This chapbook traces our responses to COVID-19 and its impact on day-to-day life—from its arrival here to the realisation that it will change society for ever.*

*This poetic collection is representative of my efforts to process and come to terms with a journey that is still ongoing. Whilst most pieces consist of simple rhymes, I've also included attempts at a few forms, namely the acrostic, duplex, haibun, haiku, interlocking rubáiyát, kyrielle, madrigal, monotetra, rondeau, sonnet and the strambotto.*

*Moreover, it is a joy to let you know that a few of these pieces have been selected to appear in anthologies, including fundraisers for charities that I still continue to support. They are: They Can't Cancel Spring in The Book of Hope and In Which Poetry Breathes Life; Healthcare Angels in The Book of Hope; Poltergeist Heist in What the Moon was Told by Dempsey & Windle; Hair Today in What Next? by Dempsey & Windle; An Unwelcome Guest in The Poetrygram Annual: 2020 and Who's Zoomin' Who? in Open Door Poetry Magazine and on the Poetry and Covid website, an international Arts and Humanities Research Council project.*

*As we enter the second lockdown here in the U.K., I hope that my shared observations may bring you comfort and encouragement as well as make you smile a little.*

*Thank you for reading.*
*I wish you and your loved ones only the very best!*

# Table Of Contents

**A. Part 1 - The Longest Journey**..........................1

1. The Longest Journey...........................................2
2. Addressing Fear..................................................3
3. Flower Power......................................................4
4. Rhyme for Mankind.............................................5
5. Wildlife Reclaims the Cities................................6
6. Coronavirus Nursery Rhyme..............................7
7. They Can't Cancel Spring...................................8
8. Missing Mums Day..............................................9
9. Cages of Glass...................................................10
10. Healthcare Angels...........................................11
11. Cora (the Goldie)'s Contented........................12
12. Doug the Destroyer.........................................13
13. A Stoic's View..................................................14

**B. Part 2 - Beneath The Surface**......................15

14. Beneath the Surface........................................16
15. CORONA–Stay In.............................................18
16. Insomania........................................................19
17. The Farewell Thief...........................................20
18. The Death of Flowers......................................21
19. Pickers who are Stickers, Please....................22
20. The Year of the Rat.........................................23
21. Finding myself.................................................24
22. Poltergeist's Heist............................................25

23. Lockdown Learnings.........................................26
24. Staying Home..................................................27

**C. Part 3 - A Tight Predicament**......................28
25. A Tight Predicament........................................29
26. It's all about Face............................................30
27. Hair Today.......................................................31
28. When we were More........................................32
29. Who's Zoomin' Who? ......................................33
30. Antisocial Distancing.......................................34
31. Dancing in Quicksand......................................35
32. Fear Festival....................................................36
33. An Unwelcome Guest......................................37
34. Washday..........................................................38
35. Living with Death in the Garden......................39

Part 1
# THE LONGEST JOURNEY

*Sharron Green © Photography*

# 1. The Longest Journey

From humble beginnings,
humongous ambition
propelled me to launch
on this deadly mission.

Far East to Wild West,
chill North to Deep South,
my home is yours too—
I live hand to mouth.

My path is a riddle
with many connections,
whilst they are unbroken,
I cause more infections.

I love to explore,
it fills me with glee—
my invisible cloak,
will always be key.

The longest journey
to so many lands;
where I go next
is out of your hands.

## 2. Addressing Fear

We met soon after Christmas,
at the turning of the year.
You first appeared upon the news
and seemed so far from here.

Yet now you are in England,
mad keen to get inside me.
I'd be flattered if it wasn't that,
you clearly can't abide me.

Covid-19 is your name,
and you're a fan of grime.
You'd like me to be dirty,
so I'm scrubbing all the time.

I wish that you did not exist,
I hate the harm you've done,
you've caused so much destruction
and there's clearly more to come.

I try to think there will be good
emerging from these times
but even if there is Covid,
I won't forgive your crimes.

## 3. Flower Power
*(a Welsh Sonnet)*

Meadow flower, forest glade,
high in jungle's canopy.
There the planet's breath is made—
drawing, delving, deep and free.
On those airways this Ark sails;
block them and our life-blood fails.
Forest filters, fight for me.

Bush fires, flooding, drought and storms,
weather's morphed to horror show.
Winds wage war, defying norms,
structures fall and systems slow.
Now we are with virus vexed—
what on Earth will happen next?
Meadow flower, heal your foe.

## 4. Rhyme for Mankind
*(a Sonnet)*

For better or worse, how will it change us?
Or will we return to the status quo?
If we don't change, we will be to blame cuz
nature's allowing a reset to 'Go'.

Life before March has been put on hold now;
let's pause and take stock of all we hold dear.
A space to unwind, pick up some know-how,
breathe in the fresh air, now that it's so clear.

It's not through our choice, no one would wish this
and certainly, it's not 'me-time' for all
but for life on Earth—flora to fishes,
it so needs to be a rallying call.

*Our goals must be steady, no longer vague.*
*What must we do to avoid the next plague?*

# 5. Wildlife Reclaims the Cities
*(my version of a Haibun)*

Slinking out, I sense a perfect peace
like I've never known before.

Pure air purges my soul,
lungs clear of the belch of metal boxes.
The tinnitus thump of my heart calms…
I tune into the birds,
bees and fellow foragers—
all now freed
from fear and repression.

How to teach my cubs the strange of this?
Lesson 1: Terror of the tarmac road
—'Fake news!' they cry
Lesson 2: Not to linger in the now long lawn—
'Chillax Mum!'
Lesson 3: Food bins must be scavenged in seconds—
'But if we eat slowly, we digest better!'

Overnight,
life skills turn into modern history.
Game changer,
we have all advanced,
promoted
to a better quality of life.
Safe distancing and home schooling
soon obsolete for us.

I am reborn with the young
who do not know they are born.
Long live this liberation—
a miracle so sorely needed.

*Nature orders in—*
*wildlife reclaims the cities;*
*shock when lockdown ends.*

# 6. Coronavirus Nursery Rhyme

Way back in early 2020
a virus came attacking plenty;
said to have started in bat poo—
a very nasty strain of flu.

It travelled swiftly round the world
and everywhere chaos unfurled.
It seemed to prey on the unwell
but even young ones couldn't smell.

It was extremely autocratic
enlisting the asymptomatic
to blithely share its spiky crop—
most countries quickly shut up shop.

In lockdown, families loved and loathed,
sprouted hair and zoomed half clothed.
Parents worked from home and taught
as jobs were lost their nerves grew fraught.
Many brave workers were still key—
they got claps, not PPE.

When it was up to every nation
to open doors and stop stagnation
they told them "Be alert", not dense,
but commonly most lacked good sense-
so desperate to meet with mates,
forgetting it could seal their fates.

The only way to halt infection
was to develop an injection,
but by the time that had been done,
the bats had shat another one!

# 7. They Can't Cancel Spring

They've cancelled the Olympics, football and tennis too.
They've called off all the festivals and parties are taboo.
But remember that the good news is they cannot cancel Spring.
Look out now from your cages and you'll see it's in full swing!

The daffs are bouncing open and the birds are warming up.
The flower show has started and the tulips want the cup.
The daisies row across the lawn with dandelions ahead.
There's clearly no safe distancing down in the flower bed!

The Spring is here to cheer us up, and doing it in style.
The virus will not block it from going the extra mile.
With front row seats and Easter treats we get to see it all.
Each day the matinee is fab, right to the curtain call!

*Remember, they can't cancel Spring so let's breathe in its bliss.*
*And count our blessings that it's here, to help us conquer this!*

# 8. Missing Mums Day

To all the mums on Mother's Day
who are in isolation:
please know we'd love to be with you,
while on this great staycation.

Thanks so much for all you've done,
to get us where we are.
We feel so sad these greetings
must reach you from afar.

Stay safe inside, be cosy,
watch TV's Mary Berry,
have a cuppa and a slice of cake,
or maybe, a large sherry?

Imagine we are there with you,
although you must confess—
at least with virtual gatherings,
there is a lot less mess!

This is a real crisis,
but when it does abate
the hugs you'll get will be so tight
as we all celebrate!

## 9. Cages of Glass
*(a Sonnet)*

In cages of glass, we hide in plain sight
from a sickness unfettered by borders.
Sadly we don't have the power to fight
so we all must obey 'stay home' orders.

As the framework of daily life shatters,
work life is home life, we must not commute.
We have time to reflect on what matters,
saving the good stuff before we reboot.

Outside the virus roams free, striking all—
wealth and status provide no protection.
Key workers heeding society's call
plead that we stop spreading infection.

*In cages of glass, we ogle at screens
trying to grasp what the hell this all means.*

# 10. Healthcare Angels

Wings outspread to wrap around us—
exhausted, flagging, vulnerable;
battling this mortal virus
that has come to hunt us all.

Brave does not begin to sum
arise the strength inside your core,
for there is not a single one,
who knows exactly what's in store.

Our task is but to stay at home,
stop the spread, reverse the trend,
until the virus cannot roam,
until it meets its own dead end.

You've always been the unsung heroes,
forgotten in our day to day,
it wasn't 'til this mighty fear rose,
that we found the words to say—
*"Healthcare Angels we give thanks,*
*for risking all to save our lives,*
*when this is done we'll raid the banks,*
*and make sure that you're recognised."*

# 11. Cora (the Goldie)'s Contented

My name is Cora, I'm just over one,
I'm such a good girl and also great fun.

I love to go out, gambolling free,
greeting all humans and dogs that I see.

Everyone's home now, 24/7
it really is my idea of heaven.

We go out for walks, sometimes a few,
the neighbours are keen to exercise too.

I'm not sure what's happened, but seriously,
whatever it is, it's ok with me!

## 12. Doug the Destroyer

My home is strewn with corpses
of boxes disembowelled
and floors where rugs once neatly lay
are now mud splashed and towelled.

The flowerbeds are trampled,
the lawn dotted with poo,
low hanging twigs have been detached—
boy, can that puppy chew!

The furniture now rearranged
to protect the coffee table
as that's where little Doug will climb
as soon as he is able.

This upside down sees shoes on high
to save them from his gnawing
and cushions put away by day
'cause they can't take the pawing.

In corners, there are toys,
bedraggled little clumps
waiting to be shredded,
or boisterously humped.

One thing's for sure, our lockdown lull's
now in the distant past
we'll savour Dougie's puppy days
knowing they too, won't last.

## 13. A Stoic's View
*(a Rondeau)*

A stoic's view, though nothing new,
could hold the key to all you do.
As ancient as philosophy,
it challenges and sets you free,
a way to see this crisis through.

So to your inner self be true,
and follow nature's steadfast cue,
stay positive and aim to see—
*a stoic's view.*

If in your garden no fear grew
but strength, control and patience too
plus wisdom in adversity—
you'd know 'what will be will be
and your response is up to you'—
*a stoic's view.*

## Part 2
# Beneath The Surface

*Sharron Green © Photography*

## 14. Beneath the Surface

A sunny morning, feeders' rammed,
tits and robins blithely land.
Crows and squirrels scare them off,
then settle down to have a scoff.

*Watching them, I can't get mad,
their interactions make me glad.*

I like to exercise with Joe,
often just on catch-up though.
He's helping everyone stay fit,
I'm sure I really look a twit.

*Each day, we crowd into his space
the best bit is his smiling face.*

To keep in touch, I might try Zoom,
and call long distance from my room.
Sometimes I find it quite intense,
the pressure to project, immense.

*It's hard to get a natural flow—
short and sweet's the way to go.*

Around midday, I catch the news,
experts keen to air their views,
scenes of hardship and despair,
with videos of cities bare.

*I calmly dip my toast in soup,
my mind is whirring in a loop.*

I pop out for my daily walk,
I miss my friends, their cheery talk.
Giving others lots of space,
I seldom see a smiling face.

*Feels strange, but clearly with good reason,
masks will be the trend this season.*

I've lots to do, I must confess,
the spare room is an awful mess.
Being a hoarder's my life's bane,
deciding what to chuck, a pain.

*I sit and sift, the 'keep' pile grows,
I hide it under chenille throws.*

Darkness falls, it's time for fun,
I pack away what I've not done.
Time for a gin or maybe wine,
time to imagine all is fine.

*Beneath the surface, staying home,
swaddled in a twilight zone.*

## 15. CORONA–Stay In
*(an Acrostic and Mesostitch)*

Couch is calling coaxingly,
outside the sky is blue.
Relax, embrace simplicity—
opportunity springs new.
Now's a time for mindfulness
and writing poems too!

## 16. Insomania
*(an Interlocking Rubaiyat)*

At dawn, I wake from shallow sleep,
veined eyes, half-lidded, sunken deep.
Raw, demi-dreams grant no respite,
despair makes camp and worries creep.

Lost minutes limp through day to night,
relinquish life, extinguish light.
This sinking sand of sweet regret,
as worry wrinkles map my plight.

A petty pattern is stone set,
my memory switched to forget.
To harvest rest, recharge, delete,
these basic needs remain unmet.

My mind plays tricks and tries to cheat,
mistrusting strangers when we meet.
And then of course anxiety,
too much for this soul to defeat.

I sacrifice sobriety,
a bid to set my demons free
and in so doing, simply be
suspended from reality.

## 17. The Farewell Thief

After all you've been through,
the lows as well as highs—
we will dearly miss you
and feel robbed of our goodbyes.

You battled for so long
and your willpower was great—
but this virus is too strong,
it's the cruelty we hate.

Both a coward and a thief,
picking those with the least fight—
part of the lasting grief
is we couldn't hug you tight.

But at least now you're at rest
and can look down from above—
you know we did our best
and our hearts are filled with love.

## 18. The Death of Flowers
*(a Sonnet)*

A flower's fate confronts it from the start,
as each bud blooms into its neighbour's shade.
First playing the adoring sibling's part,
then watching as her prom dress starts to fade.

This virus blighting childhood, halting studies,
robs dates to buttonhole or clutch bouquet.
Pricks dreams, prunes plans, segregates from buddies—
we pray those missing out will have their day.

In death, young flowers come to show respect,
their vibrancy reminds us of the past.
Now masking missing mourners, they collect
and bow in sorrow, wilting at the task.

*The death of flowers haunts them in their prime
but worse is when they never get to shine.*

# 19. Pickers who are Stickers, Please

Today Prince Charles launched an appeal
so farmers' fears must be for real.
To stop fruit crops going to waste,
they must be harvested in haste.

This year's pickers number few,
they can't get here from the EU.
Maybe workers on furlough
will sign up to have a go?

'Pick for Britain' is the urge
in the hope, there'll be a surge.
Harking back to World War Two
and jobs the Land Army would do.

The graft is hard, they must be fit,
free to commit and not just quit
because it will not be a breeze—
just 'Pickers who are Stickers,' please.

*One thing's for sure, I have a hunch—
you couldn't pick a better bunch!*

## 20. The Year of the Rat
*(a Kyrielle)*

Unlike the plagues of yesteryear,
rodents this time are in the clear,
but it has not brought them much cheer.

*It's been a bumpy year for rats.*

At first, things were a little tight,
with rest'rants closing overnight,
no one bewailed their hungry plight.

*It's been a bumpy year for rats.*

But they are such resourceful chaps,
they packed their bags to search for scraps,
so households had to set some traps.

*It's been a bumpy year for rats.*

Established now out in the sticks,
they clean up after our picnics,
resourceful, they have learnt new tricks.

*It's been a bumper year for rats.*

## 21. Finding myself

I've read and written lots about the value of this time,
how it can be so precious - so here's how I've found mine.
It certainly has potential for improving life and health,
this is a list of all the things I've learnt about myself…

I'm finding myself lazy, I really can't be arsed
to get up in the morning and do the simplest task.
I'm finding myself greedy, my sweet tooth lacks restraint,
I'm eating so much chocolate I'm starting to feel faint.

I'm finding myself thirsty, and sadly not just tea
will quench the fire, the gin desire that's raging inside me.
I'm finding myself hairy, my bob has gone to pot,
and bristles keep on sprouting, from places they should not.

I'm finding myself boring and lockdown is to blame
I try to think of something new but each day is the same.
I'm finding myself lardy, my scales laugh with derision
my gym time is now squandered on watching television.

I'm finding myself tearful, sensitive and sometimes down,
I suppose it's not surprising with this virus all around.
*I'm hoping someday soon, when we are Covid-free,*
*the return of social contact will help me find the real me.*

## 22. Poltergeist Heist

I'm partial to a drop of gin
especially if it's pink.
I team it with some lemonade
and it's down in a blink.

Lately, it's been going
at quite a rapid pace.
It seems there's another runner
in the spirit quaffing race.

Last night at gin o'clock,
I thought I'd draw a line
along the level in the bottle
just after I'd poured mine.

To my surprise this morning,
there's been another heist
I'm going to tell my husband
that we've got a poltergeist!

But just before I do that,
I'll check the bottle shelf,
to see if any others
have been pilfered by the elf.

That's funny, there's no vodka,
I think that is a sign—
my hubby's tipple's finished
and he's tucking into mine!

## 23. Lockdown Learnings

I feel relieved, the Earth has breathed,
our local wildlife's been reprieved.
I'm glad there's proof it can be done,
if we all compromise as one.

With diaries and schedules free,
for some reduced anxiety.
Now exercise and diet may
become the focus of our day.

As basically we've no excuse
not to have ditched our self-abuse.
Staying at home helps us connect,
with neighbours we used to neglect.

We've learnt to live communally
and value what abounds for free.
This pause for creativity
will have inspired great works to be.

My hope is that when lockdown ends
we and the planet can be friends.
The checks and pauses we have seen,
can help us keep our airways clean.

*For otherwise, what has it taught
if sacrifices were for nought?*

## 24. Staying Home
*(a Monotetra and Monorhyme)*

Lockdown meant plans were suspended,
countless hopes and dreams upended,
videos and cartoons trended…
*Some offended! Some offended!*

Pretty soon the days all blended,
walls were painted, gardens tended,
many things were made or mended…
*Neighbours friended! Neighbours friended!*

# Part 3
# A Tight Predicament

*Sharron Green © Photography*

## 25. A Tight Predicament

My underwear, has gone somewhere!
I don't know where it's gone.
The drawers are bare, there's nothing spare,
what's left, feels put upon.

The wardrobe's staged a sit in,
all comfy clothes on strike,
my going out are wearing thin,
I can't dress how I'd like.

I feel adrift 'tween sizes,
already going large,
I'll know the hell, of XXL,
if I don't soon take charge.

I'm blaming it on lockdown,
a lack of exercise,
no outings to dress up for,
too many shepherd's pies.

In truth, I should be keener,
the latest masks to model,
with luck, I won't be recognised
as round the shops I waddle!

## 26. It's all about Face
*(my version of a Duplex)*

Not long ago, our faces could be bare
and we could enter shops without a care.

Now entrances to shops instruct 'take care'
and bare-faced patrons are subject to glares.

So staff admonish customers with glares
(although they're mask exempt when stacking wares).

Some claim they have forgot, caught unawares
but there's the chance to stock up then on spares.

For different outfits now I keep some spares
(a tip would be to buy mask-maker shares).

It's best to keep masks clean and avoid shares
in order to suppress all Covid scares.

It's only since the dawn of Covid scares—
not long ago our faces could be bare.

## 27. Hair Today

I had a tidy bob, cut into the neck
shaved down to the hairline,
uniform of bejowled matrons.
After a jagged, neither-nor phase—
now cheerfully curling up,
collar-surfing.
I'll not go that short again.

Thin silver streaks flourish,
cover blown.
Dye delayed,
I pretend they are sun-kissed.
Free foils.
Shall I stay natural?
Be my colour,
before I'm no colour?

The boys have had kitchen scissor cuts.
Okay for video calls
but back and sides hacked,
mangy, deranged asylum-detained.

When salons swoosh open,
I will wait
while they brush up on
dormant skills.

It will be bizarre, BYO magazine
maybe biscuit & coffee too.
No holiday small talk,
just lockstalgia,
'What haven't you done lately?'
'Did your neighbours clap?'
as the corona crown
is mown down.

## 28. When we were More

*Here's to the life we led before...*

when we could stroll into a store
without a queue, and maskless too.

when trains were packed
and lifts were jammed
and people into theatres crammed.

when we could watch a TV host
and not think,
'He's a bit too close.'

when we could plan a holiday
an awaycation,
not a stay.

when gathering family in a room
didn't mean
we had to Zoom.

when greeting meant
one kiss or two
or will a hug or handshake do?

**Now all taboo.**

*Here's to a life we led before—
when we were more.*

## 29. Who's Zoomin' Who?

We're getting into zooming,
it keeps us in the loop,
it's great for virtual gatherings,
like quizzes or book group.

We sit at home, drink what we like
and wear what we want too
as long as we are fully clothed
when dashing to the loo!

Right now, for groups of over six
it is the only way,
to visit others' houses
at any time of day.

For work, it has become the norm
with meetings back to back,
there is no time for travelling
for gossip or to snack.

For those with things to hide behind
a backdrop can be fun,
unless you have a bookshelf
to show off to everyone.

Some like to be invisible
or mute, if home-life's loud.
It is our way to mingle,
far from the madding crowd!

## 30. Antisocial Distancing

So here we are
stranded on shoreless seas,
helpless and hopeless,
plans hang in the breeze.

*2020 plods stickily on,
sometimes I think,
'Will it ever be gone'?*

Deep sorrow lingers
for lost ones held dear,
compounded by trauma,
haunted by fear.

Wearied by waves,
befuddled by change,
dates that we make,
ditch, and then rearrange.

Milestones we're missing
and life we can't live
captured in stasis
like gold in a sieve.

What filters through
is placid, diluted;
when will our days switch
to colour from muted?

*Are we too social, do we need to unfriend?
Without isolation will we not mend?
When Zoom is the way to see your big brother
how can society ever recover?*

## 31. Dancing in Quicksand

Aeons ago, we came to the ball—
a nightmare from which there's no leaving.
Like a stuck record, we spin in a groove,
so dizzy now that we're heaving.

The ballroom once splendid is tarnished,
the crystal and gold have been scuffed.
In our finest we stood, eating all that we could
and now it's all gone, we are stuffed.

The band plays a Titanic medley
as chairs round the dance floor swap places,
the ball gowns bob, in the bubbling mud
and we stare at the horrified faces.

What we need is a Fairy Godmother
to whisk us back with a gaze so adoring
to the days when our planet was healthy
and our politics simple and boring.

## 32. Fear Festival

*The haunted house is screaming doom*
*as witches spittle in the gloom.*

Plague rats are primed,
cobwebs are draped,
Bleached vampires fanged
and velvet caped.

Gaunt ghosts are coughing,
dragging chains
while graves lay waiting
for remains.

Bat blood is curdling
in a pool,
the temperature
is far from cool.

So will kids still shout
'Trick or Treat'?
and dare they knock
to swipe a sweet?

*The stage is set for Halloween,*
*this year's the scariest we've seen.*

## 33. An Unwelcome Guest
*(a Strambotto)*

Back in mid-Winter, with a cold steady grip,
news spread from the East and was all about you.

In Spring, you bounced in with a hop and a skip,
you were green, fresh and keen, how little we knew.

The Summer sun blazed and we gave you the slip
in pubs and on beaches your mingling grew.

Now heading to Autumn, as trees start to strip,
we wish that you'd go but you're sticking like glue.

## 34. Washday
*(a Madrigal)*

Each day we have's unique in ev'ry way.
The setting of the sun brings joy and pain.
We spin within a force that we can't tame.

Our golden orb descends, it cannot stay.
Sky washing as it wends all shades of flame.
Each day, we have's unique in ev'ry way.
The setting of the sun brings joy and pain.

Milestones leave merry marks, as they sashay.
Dull doubts and raw regrets in ash remain.
Our task—cleanse and refresh, learn from each stain.
Each day we have's unique in ev'ry way.
The setting of the sun brings joy and pain.
We spin within a force that we can't tame.

## 35. Living with Death in the Garden
*(my version of a Blues Sonnet)*

The season we call Autumn's also Fall.
We weep as golden leaves begin to fall,
then sweep them in a heap against the wall.

The sky says 'Bye' to days of dazzling blue
and under its grey mantle I feel blue,
but blunder round the garden—lots to do.

Time now to prune the roses, leave beds bare,
and feel, wrapped in that process, thoughts laid bare—
entrusting tulip bulbs to nature's care.

Beneath the frozen earth, everything's still.
With grief, devoid of mirth, we're busy still—
a wreath of Christmas holly stabs the chill.

*Just when we're feeling trapped in Winter's death,
a hint of Summer's warmth lives in Spring's breath.*

*Sharron Green © Photography*

# Acknowledgements

First and foremost, I would like to thank Kevin and Sam for their patient support and to Dougie for walking with me as I composed my rhymes.

A special thank you to Rita & Dick who inspired Who's Zoomin' Who?
I'm grateful to my friends at the Poetix University @poetixu team—Tonii, Dara, Nupur & Ahja—for their encouragement, great workshops & books.

A sincere note of thanks to Reena Doss and Ink Gladiators Press for their expertise and companionship on this journey to publication.

I've been writing rhyming poems ever since I was a child but only began posting them on social media from June 2019 onwards. I've been so grateful for the vibrant poetry community who have consistently supported, inspired and challenged me to keep on writing, particularly the following accounts:

@aefoxx | @a.j.butler.poetry | @alexialeighwrites | @amykaypoetry
@bybtpoetrysupport | @captain_subtle | @confessions_of_sophia
@electricarmchair | @eve_poetry | @heathermoulson | @kaliskamera
@kingdomherrmann | @ladyleighpoetry | @lindalokheeauthor
@l.t.pelle | @lutra.luna | @myth.and.lore | @opendoorpoetrymagazine
@penandpendulum | @pen_pals_writings | @poemsbyalwyn
@poems_by_tessy_live | @poetconnection @poetrybattles
@poetryolympics | @randomerbobsxyz | @rupikaur
@sarahdrury_artandpoetry | @shandrewspoetry | @sharrons_writing
@the_book_of_hope | @thedancingink | @thegridbeatsstrong
@themumpoempress | @thetasteofmypen | @tonii2eyes
@twisted.word.tango | @weloveglobalpoets | @witchesnbtches
@writer_in_residence | @writingpoemsinthedark

Thank you very much,

@rhymes_n_roses

# ABOUT THE AUTHOR

Sharron Green is a published poet with two of her own chapbooks as well as several poems appearing in over ten anthologies. She began writing poetry to make sense of modern life and loves experimenting with rhymes and poetic forms. She is also a passionate nature and flower photographer with roses occupying a special place in her heart. These elements have been incorporated into her public persona and are how she came to be known as the Rhymes and Roses Queen.

Sharron currently lives in Guildford, England and is studying for an MA in Creative Writing at the University of Surrey. There she is working on several writing projects that she looks forward to sharing in the future.

*Scan the QR code below to visit Sharron Green at www.rhymesnroses.com*

*Find her on Instagram and Facebook @rhymes_n_roses*
*Email her at rhymesnrosespoetry@gmail.com.*

# Tell Us What You Think

Write to us at contact@inkgladiatorspress.com.
We might add your comments or reviews on our website
as well as feature your Instagram profile.
We appreciate your love for reading.

Thank you!

We remain at your service,
Reena Doss | Founder
Ink Gladiators Press®
**www.inkgladiatorspress.com**

*"Hi," cooed the peace dove,
through the windows of the cage,
"from nature with love."*